Descending Fire

Jean Petit

Descending Fire

The Journal of a Soul Aflame

SOPHIA INSTITUTE PRESS®
Manchester, New Hampshire

Sophia Institute Press®
Box 5284, Manchester, NH 03108
1-800-888-9344
www.sophiainstitute.com

Nihil obstat: André Combes, *Censor deputatus*
Imprimatur: Michael Potevin, Vicar General
Paris, April 25, 1953

Library of Congress Cataloging-in-Publication Data

Petit, Jean.
    Descending fire : the journal of a soul aflame / Jean Petit.
        p.   cm.
    Abridgement of: Le feu qui descend. 1953.
    Includes bibliographical references.
    ISBN 1-928832-23-7 (pbk. : alk. paper)
    1. Thérèse, de Lisieux, Saint, 1873-1897. 2. Christian saints —
France — Lisieux — Biography. I. Petit, Jean. Feu qui descend.
English. II. Title.

BX4700.T5 P45 2001
248.2'2 — dc21   2001020188

02 03 04 05 06 07 10 9 8 7 6 5 4 3 2

Preface

＊

There are things our author cannot say himself and which prompt us to add a few lines of our own.

The pseudonymous Jean Petit is a priest and one who would never have dreamed of having his notes published if we had not prevailed upon him to do so. It was only on condition that we take upon ourselves the full responsibility of their publication and allow his identity to remain unknown that he finally acquiesced to hand over to us the pages you are about to read.

Dom Vincent Artus, O.S.B.
Abbey of St.-André-lez-Bruges
September 15, 1952

Publisher's note

꙼

As Fr. Artus just noted, the French edition of *Descending Fire* is a selection of notes and journal entries written over the years by the pseudonymous Fr. Jean Petit. Among these writings are sublime renderings of the passionate work of God in our souls, as well as sometimes dry commentaries on certain phrases by St. Thérèse of Lisieux, on passages in Scripture, and on a number of feast days in the Church.

Because our purpose in these pages is merely to introduce the thought of Fr. Petit to English-speaking readers, we do not include here all of Fr. Petit's notes from the original French edition, but rather put before you those that contain the core of what he has seen.

Descending Fire

This first abridged English translation is, then, just a beginning. At a later date, once Jean Petit is better known, others more accomplished than we can produce a complete and scholarly edition of *Le Feu qui Descend*.

Until then, dwell in these pages, and pray that through them the fire may descend into your soul and set it aflame like the soul of Jean Petit.

Author's preface

⚮

The following pages are from my personal journal, into which I tried to inject a little order. They tell of an experience, of a certain period in my life. Do not, then, expect a methodical study where there is none. The order that I have tried to introduce is more apparent than real. You cannot cut into a segment of life without risking severe consequences. Just as a man keeps finding himself in each of his acts, so each of the following pages contains all the others. Therefore, there will be repetitions, but they will never cease to remind us of the unique meaning which is the real reason behind these notes.

Fr. Jean Petit

Descending Fire

From the age of fifteen, around the year 1911, my soul has been filled with irresistible desires. They take hold of me and draw me on in spite of myself, even on bad days. I feel an immense need to pray for the accomplishment of the divine plan of creation, Incarnation, and Redemption; a constant anxiousness for the whole Christ, for the Church Triumphant, the Church Militant, and the Church Suffering; I feel a desire for a universality of vision that cannot be limited. I see only through the eyes of Christ in His sacerdotal prayer,[1] and this is what I most desire.

[1] Cf. John 17.

This is followed by an inward assurance that one day all will be accomplished, everything will come together, and the accomplishment will be perfect. These are the facts; I note them simply.

This mystery of my soul never ceases to amaze me, and the same question is always rising from my heart and lips: "Why . . . ?"

Why? Why these calls, these inward tendencies, these lights that were inspired not by the writings of St. Thomas Aquinas, nor by St. John of the Cross, nor by St. Thérèse's book?[2] The voice of the soul, the little lamp that is never extinguished, has come before every idea ever recorded in books; and I have not consulted the teachings of the saints to be assured of the orthodoxy of my tendencies.

Theology has made me understand how prayer, far from changing God's plans, brings them about. It makes us see in time what God has decreed from all

[2] The autobiography of St. Thérèse of Lisieux.

eternity that we should ask Him. The Divine Munificence has decided from all eternity to bring into harmony whatever it urges me to ask for in this world. St. Thérèse of Lisieux understood this when she wrote, "The more You wish to give, the more You make us desire."

The day I understood these truths, I had made great strides, and the *why*s in my life fell away from me. The light that, with various degrees of intensity, is always shining in the depths of my being is now truly the light of the Divine Word. The voice that speaks to me without noise is that of my Creator. The hidden fire that does not cease to consume me, the hand — at once so gentle and so firm — that guides me in darkness, and the magnet that continuously draws me are truly Jesus Himself: Light, Voice, Fire, and Magnet.

Finally, I have understood that it is impossible to confine my prayer to time and space. I have found in this a spiritual vocation.

Descending Fire

Although I have been drawn to the Infinite since 1911, it is mainly from 1943 that there has been transformation in my soul. The last words that I made note of in July 1945, before leaving M—, were these: "You were supernaturally happy at M— because it was there that you experienced the Holy Trinity; it was there that you made contact with Divinity; it was there that you touched God."

Truly, especially since November 1943, I have touched Divinity. God communicates Himself to me without my embracing Him; He shows Himself without my seeing Him; He speaks to me without my hearing Him. I do not see Him; I do not hear Him. Yet He speaks to me and shows Himself to me. At each moment, He communicates Himself. Without hearing Him, I know what He is saying. Just as He does not speak to me in human language, so I cannot put into words what He makes me understand. I know only that I possess Him, that He is everything to me, that at each moment He penetrates me, and in the same measure my life disappears in Him. One day I will be totally permeated by Him to the point where I will no longer be myself; my being will be transformed into the flame of the Holy Spirit. That flame, uniformly spread out over many wretched souls, will be diffused throughout the world until the plan of creation, Incarnation, and Redemption is brought to full realization; in other words, until the Lord's Prayer and the sacerdotal prayer are brought to fulfillment.

❧

In Heaven, the elect bear a new name, one conferred on them by God from all eternity. "To him who conquers I will give . . . the hidden manna, and I will give him a . . . new name."[3] This name is bestowed on the elect by Jesus, the divine Pastor: Christ calls His sheep by their proper names.[4] It corresponds to the personal grace that has been given to them by the Lord,

[3] Rev. 2:17.
[4] Cf. John 10:27.

according to the bent of their spirituality. It is the complete expression, decreed by God Himself, of their spiritual vocation.

St. Thérèse of the Child Jesus one day found in St. Paul the name that God had destined for her. In great joy, she cried out, "In the heart of the Church, my Mother, I will be *love*." She was not only vowed to Merciful Love as others are consecrated to justice, but she wanted to be identified so much with the torrents of divine fire that were overflowing in her soul that her whole being was transformed into a fiery furnace.

I, too, in my nothingness, will bring before the everlasting God the name that has become the life of my soul. The immense stream of flames descending upon man from the Trinity through the union of the divinity and the humanity in the Person of Christ will bear me along by its impetuous force, will destroy in me what remains of my self, will change me little by little into Himself, will make me disappear into His unfathomable mystery, and what remains of me will

be fashioned into a new being that will still be me,
yet no longer me, a creature swallowed up in the consuming fires of divinity.

I will be merciful love.

That is my name. That is my signature. It is the
only truth, since that is the only thing that counts
before God.

꧂

I know, then, the name I will bear when I appear
before God. My other name will have disappeared.
Like me and with me, it will be buried, lost, consumed,
transformed into the abyss St. John has defined as
"Love."[5]

To what extent will divinity pervade my being? Already grace makes the *substance* of my soul divine. The
Holy Trinity abides in me — "We will make our home
with him"[6] — as in a temple: "You are God's temple."[7]

[5] Cf. 1 John 4:8.
[6] John 14:23.
[7] 1 Cor. 3:16.

Descending Fire

I participate in the divine nature.[8] I live in Christ, and Christ lives in me;[9] I no longer live anything but the life of Jesus.[10] The Holy Spirit has been given to me.[11]

"You are gods, sons of the Most High, all of you."[12] "Just as fire can make an object glow with incandescent heat," says St. Thomas, "so God can deify souls."[13]

But grace can do still more. In transforming union, it makes even the *powers* of the soul divine. Then the understanding, the will, and the memory of the soul become in some way the understanding, the will, and the memory of God.

There is still more. Beyond the substance of the soul, beyond its powers, grace can divinize its *acts* by the divine movement that has become the ordinary.

[8] Cf. 2 Pet. 1:4.
[9] Cf. John 6:56.
[10] Cf. Gal. 2:20.
[11] Cf. Rom. 5:5.
[12] Ps. 82:6.
[13] St. Thomas Aquinas (1225-1274), Dominican theologian, philosopher, and Doctor of the Church.

This last transformation is the work of the grace but, above all, of love. It is strictly the act of love.

Thérèse, with ingenious simplicity, took on the ideal to live, not only in love, but in "an act of love." In order that her acts of charity might be perfect, she desired to live not only in love, not only in perfect love, but in "a single act of perfect love." She desired to live in this single act; she desired her whole life to be this single act. To live in this unique act of perfect love, she offered herself as a victim to Merciful Love.[14]

※

One day you will have disappeared into the flames of the Infinite.

Nothingness — have you understood?

Nothingness — do you dare to understand?

You will live in the *unique act* of the One who is Charity.

---

[14]St. Thérèse's Act of Oblation to Merciful Love, on which the author comments often in these pages, is printed at the end of this book. — ED.

Descending Fire

You will be consumed in the One who is the supreme Good.

You will shine in the One who is Being.

Have you understood?

When you are tempted to forget, read again the sacerdotal prayer, which is the supreme vision of Christ before His death. It is the zenith of His whole life. One day, not only will you live this prayer, but it will be your habitual nourishment. It is complete; it is total; it consumes our being. It is completely satisfying. Nothing is lacking to it. Each time you repeat it, you will desire nothing else. It is the only thing that gives you complete peace. It is the fullness of prayer, the prayer of Jesus the Priest, the testament of the good Master: the prayer of Trinity and Unity.

⁂

To be nothing, to feel that I am nothing, to be identified with my nothingness; to love, to cherish this nothingness is one of the most fundamental inclinations of my soul. In spite of certain natural

12

repugnances and many faults, I have reached a point where I delight in humiliations and cannot do without them. This intense love of humiliation — this annihilation, if you will — has become a passion with me, a subject of joy. Despite the natural horror I have of emptiness, I search blindly for this "nothing," not for myself, but "so that the Cross of Christ will not be emptied of its power."[15] God has also given me a love for the supreme annihilation of death, that noble friend and great truth which I must face alone and which will be my last trial and final grace. Always — at least I hope — this "nothing" will be my faithful companion.

I have asked Him so fervently to make me nothingness! The God of mercy is a God who is inclined to humble Himself and to search out the wretched. The Infinite has answered and has lavished on me the grace of humiliations.

---

[15] Cf. 1 Cor. 1:17.

Descending Fire

I am not successful in any undertaking; if I render a service, it is turned against me, and all effort ends clumsily in failure. Far from being discouraged by these things, I find my joy in them. If I were so unlucky as to succeed, I would have to ask whether God loved me less or whether He wished to punish me.

This is because we cannot obtain the fullness of God without first recognizing our nothingness. I will receive God's fullness in proportion to my own annihilation, which is a response to the unspeakable annihilation of the Incarnate Word. I will be charity only to the extent to which I cease to be myself. As in a scale, the humbler I become, the higher charity can rise in me.

What form does annihilation take for me? It is found, not in grand humiliations, nor in vainglorious sufferings, nor even in ostentatious heroism, but rather in my utter inability to succeed in anything. I am powerless to find any joy or satisfaction in success. I find annihilation in the joy of feeling myself unfit and powerless.

For my part, I know that all fruit must fall heavily to the ground before reaching maturity. Nothing has succeeded for me in the past; nothing will succeed for me in the future. It will be an unhappy day for me when I feel satisfied by some result or success.

I must flow like water, vanish like the wind, melt like snow, be consumed like a candle, wither like a flower on the altar. It is my way; it is my path; it is my route. It is my whole past. It is my whole future.

I will never be strong. "Strength is made perfect in weakness."[16] Strength is my weakness, "lest the Cross of Christ be emptied of its power." If we discount weakness, what remains of the Cross? My strength is the Cross of Christ. I am lost if I glory in anything except the Cross.[17] I must never know what tomorrow will bring. I know only that tomorrow is the strength of God in the presence of my powerlessness.

[16]Cf. 2 Cor. 12:9.
[17]Cf. Gal. 6:14.

The heart of this doctrine is found in the *Magnificat*: "He who is mighty has done great things for me."[18] He who has great power in Himself can do great things in me.

If I am brought to nothingness, it will be evident that it is God who is working totally in me (while allowing the human element its place in the scheme of things). God is a jealous God.[19] He builds only on ruins, on the ruin of my self. The abyss of nothingness calls forth His mercy, and He fills it only in the measure of its emptiness. If the space is big enough, the divine Ocean of mercy will fill it entirely.

I alone cannot bring about this destruction of my self-love, but I can and must put forth the effort to cooperate in this work. God, who created me without my consent, does not wish to raise me to a share in His divine life without asking my cooperation. But my

[18]Luke 1:49.
[19]Cf. Exod. 20:5.

personal efforts are only evidence of my goodwill — efforts God waits for before acting Himself. It is the same love of God that brings to nothing and that raises up again. Thus, man will have nothing to boast about. To God alone will be given all honor and praise.

Therefore, each time I raise my heart to God, I must be imbued with my own wretchedness as well as that of all mankind. I must always remember this, implicitly at least, since it is the reason for both my hope and my assurance. My prayer will be like this:

> *O Holy Trinity,*
> *consume in your fire*
> *the misery of so many souls,*
> *and my own misery as well.*

The more we become identified with our nothingness, the more will the torrents of divine fire stream toward our nothingness. God overflows like an ocean at high tide, casting Himself into the yawning chasm. "The weaker and more wretched we are," writes St.

Thérèse of the Child Jesus, "the more we have a claim on the operations of consuming and transforming love."

God can fill the void in man only to the extent that He finds it empty. A cavern that is filled is no longer a cavern; floods cannot penetrate it.

All fatherhood, whether in Heaven or on earth, receives its fruitfulness from the fatherhood of God.[20] Everything good comes from God; nothing is brought into being without Him. This goes for the whole universe until such time as the plan of creation, Incarnation, and Redemption is accomplished; in other words, as far as His love can reach. Or again, until the fullness of Christ's Mystical Body is complete; until the Father's name is perfectly hallowed, until His kingdom comes and His will is done on earth as it is in Heaven; until the souls destined to believe in Christ eventually are made one in Him.

[20]Cf. Eph. 3:14-15.

Descending Fire

This is what is called for in the Lord's Prayer and in the sacerdotal prayer — the only two prayers that give my soul complete satisfaction and fulfill all my desires. When I try to pray for special intentions, some interior power seems to stop me, and a voice says to me, "Why do you limit the fervor of your aspiration? Why do you not let them follow their flight into time and space, outside of time and space, into the great abyss of divine eternity, wherever God wishes to be adored and loved?" Then, instinctively, I seek refuge in the two prayers of Jesus, and there my heart finds perfect peace.

From the age of eighteen, I have had a yearning to express all my prayers by one word that has become like breathing to me and that concretizes my desires: *all*. It expresses my need to neglect nothing that concerns the divine plan and to let God enlarge my heart to the measure of infinity.

The human heart that burns with divine fire is so large that the universe can fit in it. My actual sentiments are the same as when I was eighteen, but they are expressed differently now. From that time to the present, my impulse has always been the same; I constantly hear the same irresistible call, continuing on in the same direction without delay or hesitation: with and through Christ in the Eucharist, in the Spirit of the Father and the Son, my soul asks of the infinitely loving Father for that perfect unity of all predestined souls. Unity in charity between God and souls, between souls and God, and between all the souls of the elect, like that unity which exists between the Three Divine Persons, is the object of my unceasing prayer, just as it was the object of Jesus' supplication the day before He died.[21] Who else but He could express the inexpressible?

ᴥ

Fire tends naturally to transform into itself everything in its path. The flame which is the Holy Spirit seeks to reach out and envelop every object in its way.

[21]Cf. John 17:11.

Descending Fire

Such is its nature. It will spread until the love with which the Father has loved Christ is found in all pre-destined souls. This is its only limit. It is the only thing that God desires. A unique and selfsame love must unite the Father to Jesus, Jesus to the Father, the Father to souls through Jesus, and souls with each other in the Holy Spirit.

I should really pray that the love of the Holy Spirit might encompass the entire universe: all pain, the fervor of each death, the perfection of every imperfect act, the voice of all irrational creatures. Each of these could be a whole chapter in itself. Two canticles express it perfectly: the *Benedicite:* "Bless the Lord, all you works of the Lord. . . ."[22] and St. Francis of Assisi's song of the creatures.[23]

St. John of the Cross wrote that the transformed soul accomplishes its work of knowledge and love *in*

[22] Dan. 3:35-66.
[23] St. Francis of Assisi (c. 1182-1226), founder of the Franciscan Order.

the Trinity, *with* the Trinity, and *as* the Trinity itself.[24]
In one and the same movement is fulfilled the act of
charity and the fatherhood of God. The final end of
this perfect and unique act of charity and paternity
is the Holy Trinity, which is both the unparalleled
model and the unique fountainhead.

⚜

*It is amazing that these thoughts do not frighten me.
No, my God, I am not afraid of You. Your unfathomable
degree of height and depth do not stagger me. St. Thérèse
of the Child Jesus, soul of my soul, and my Mother the
Holy Virgin, and my elder Brother Jesus have all spoken
to me in words that are easily understood. I have no fear.
I cast myself into You with closed eyes, in naked faith and
naked hope.*

[24]*Canticle*, Stanza 19.

I see in the air flowers, immense roses that are flames. They fall in a burning downpour and seek out hidden refuges that wish to receive them. The heavens reflect their glow, and the lustrous skies are filled with their movement. In reality, this fire does not fall peacefully to the earth. Many reject it, refuse to receive it.[25] Those who reject it are Christians who know the gospel: millions of Catholics, schismatics, and Protestants.

Other burning clouds fill the air with their fire, but they have had a less humiliating fate. They are not rejected, but are ignored or misunderstood. These

---

[25]"His own people received Him not" (John 1:11).

clouds are the love that God reserved for the millions of infidels, pagans, Mohammedans, Jews, and other non-Christians who are unaware of the Gospel and even the name of Jesus.

But the child[26] is ready to receive this brilliant fire.

And her offering is accepted.

In this way, the child becomes love scorned and love ignored. She loves on behalf of those who reject or ignore the tenderness of the Father. She loves perfectly, not only for Catholics and separated Christians, but also in the name of all present-day unbelievers. She loves also for those who, in the past, have refused or have not recognized the Father's love; and she loves every sinner of future ages. Love poured into her soul accomplishes the eternal plan of the love of the Creator and completes the vision of redemption. She responds fully at the end of her Act of Oblation: "To make amends to God for the obstacles that His creatures

[26]Thérèse of the Child Jesus.

put in the way of that love that He wishes to lavish on them."[27]

※

I do not want to rely on appearances. I must view things as God does and judge them with His own infinite kindness. Is it true that "He has great pity when it concerns souls"? It is a pleasing phrase, but is it true? The almighty Father has spoken of the "failure of the Redemption." This is a sensational phrase. Is this also true? We know that Christ has not prayed in vain; His sacerdotal prayer will be and is being accomplished each day.

I will never forget that the victim of love loves with that same love with which Christians and non-Christians alike should love our universal Father. She makes up for what is lacking in their vocation of charity. In this manner, the plan of God's love is accomplished.

[27]*Catechism of the Act of Offering to Merciful Love*, Central Office, Lisieux.

Descending Fire

＊

— I suffer much in seeing people who do not love our Lord.

— You must not feel pain.

— ?

— Let us say you arrive in good spirits at the home of your friend X—, and you knock briskly at her door in anticipation of spending an hour in pleasant conversation with her. She opens the door, looks at you with scorn, and closes the door in your face. You are hurt, and you go to recount your experience to Z—, who is eager to prepare coffee to your liking while she offers you cakes, pralines, and candy and keeps you until midnight to give you that sense of joy and warmth which you had previously been refused. You return home filled with happiness. A friend has welcomed your companionship, which had been rejected elsewhere.

— . . . .

— Let us now apply this to God. He knocks at the door of your unbelieving neighbor, who refuses to offer

Him hospitality even at the insistence of divine friend-ship. Will you spend your time fretting and grieving about it? I hope you will be more practical and take a decisive step, saying to God, "Here is my heart. Place in it the fire You wanted to conceal in the soul of my neighbor." God will be content. His love will have found a refuge.

But the Creator knocks also at the door of Y— . If He is refused the hospitality of that house, say then to our heavenly Father, "Let my heart be the sanctuary of that love which Y— rejects also."

A great many people rudely scorn the paternal ten-derness of God. Do not spend time bewailing the fact, but open wide your soul for these people who reject the light. In this way, the Blessed Trinity will find there the love that It had anticipated.

— . . . ?

— When the divine fire descends in you with the Holy Spirit, it takes refuge in your soul, at the same time enveloping and moving it. It is the container and the contained. It is not subject to the physical laws of the recipient. It moves in you, and you are moved in it. You encompass it, and at the same time you are surrounded by its greatness. With the Three Divine Persons who live in you, the infinite fire is more at ease if it finds a soul that lacks confidence in itself. That is what it is looking for. This torrent of love asks only to descend and to rush in with a force proportionate to the depths of your lowliness. Ask our heavenly Father to create in you a childlike heart completely open to the action of His tenderness. He will lean toward your soul and will prepare it to become an ocean of flames.

— . . . .

— Prepare yourself to receive the fire that Jesus has come to bring to the earth and that He wishes to be kindled.[28] A burning shower will engulf you. The waves will press in upon you like so many tongues of fire. They will be alive and bearers of life; they will be

[28]Cf. Luke 12:49.

active and overflowing with fruitfulness. They will burn you; they will consume you; they will crush your earthly shell until the day . . .

— Until the day . . . ?

— Until that blessed day when they will break down your resistance, when they will overpower the feeble strength of your body and will restore your immortal soul to its first fervor kindled by the feeble spark springing from uncreated goodness and transformed into a consuming fire. For you, this will be the day of martyrdom through love. Your heart will no longer be able to support the weight of the ocean. Your life will not necessarily be shortened; but instead of being brought to an end by a natural cause, your last hour will be a death through love.

— . . . !

— That is what happened to St. Thérèse of the Child Jesus. If you are surprised by the boldness of her ideas, do not forget that she is "the greatest saint of modern times." Are you afraid to follow her to the end? She thought especially of you when she asked God to "raise up a legion of little souls," capable of loving Him and of making Him loved perfectly.

— She thought of me?

— Yes, she thought of you when she formulated the desire to share with many humble and confident hearts the happiness of "living in a single act of perfect love." For love to be perfect, for it to be a single act, and for this act to unite with your life itself, it is necessary that this tenderness be the tenderness of God and the loving soul be consumed in the burning life of the Blessed Trinity. Such is the privilege that the young Carmelite of Lisieux begged for herself on June 9, 1895[29] and which she also requested for you.

— For me?

— Does this alarm you? Are you afraid to get too close to her? Do you not dare to allow your heart to expand? Are you a child of the Church? Do you

[29]The date of St. Thérèse's Act of Self Oblation.

believe in God's divine paternity? God has given you a father and a mother who are for you the symbol of boundless love. Suppose you had behaved very badly one day. Your parents may not have slept and would have asked each other, "What can we do to make this child become better?" So much the more will our heavenly Father, who alone is good,[30] do everything for you and go to great lengths to call you back from your rashness.

Like the extraordinary child of Lisieux, you must love perfectly for those who do not love and for those who do not love enough.

[30]Cf. Mark 10:18.

＊

The Creator has concealed in the universe many powerful forces that have an impact on our soul and awaken in it awe: the fury of the storm and of the ocean, the mystery of the chasm and of the mountain, the explosion of the atom. But the creature itself should be for us a sign of more hidden wonders; and the great manifestations of nature announce to us more moving secrets. The contemplation of these things can leave the soul mystified. It is the divine fire invading the world.

＊

The first scene: Whether I cast my eyes to the right or to the left, raise them on high or cast them down, I discover the Infinite all about me — the Infinite who is the Father, the Infinite who is the Thought of the

Descending Fire

Father, the Infinite who is the reciprocal love of the Father and His Thought; the Infinite "in which I live and move and have my being."[31] This reciprocal love, since it is fire, burns extensively and transforms into itself anything that is not an obstacle to this love. Since it is a merciful fire, it wants to descend, to diffuse itself all around, to be reduced to poverty, to fill the emptiness of our souls, and to act for us. The Infinite rushes in with such impetuosity that the creature becomes more conscious of its own powerlessness. This is the law of contrasts. Acceptance of our misery determines the extent to which we receive this flaming torrent.

There are, then, three oceans: *the Infinite*, which represents the life of the Blessed Trinity; *the utter poverty* of the creature who is waiting, and, between these two, *a burning shower* that spreads out, wanting to engulf the universe.

[31]Cf. Acts 17:28.

⁂

The second scene: The fire of the Most High seeks, then, to invade the heart of man, whose depth has been determined by the Infinite and whose dimensions have been determined in the light of Immensity itself.

The torrent is at the door of our heart, which remains closed. Like the water that crashes on rocks and rises up like plumes of foam, these burning waves clash against our refusal, rearing up in leaps, then descending only to rise again. They are there pressing impatiently. Will they go away without finding a welcome?

In order to stem the tide, people unite to raise barricades. The roaring sea only becomes more majestic, its waves reaching to the stars, its voice reaching to God . . . until, perhaps, God grows tired?

Of course not; that is not possible. A single spark of fatherly tenderness cannot remain without a response.

⁂

The third scene: In prehistoric times, when the floods made hollows in the valley, the waters clashed against the rocks, forming the landscape that we see today; and after many meanderings, they succeeded in carving an outlet for themselves. All the rivers followed this course, and each drop of water fulfilled its destiny.

In much the same way, the torrent of divine flames will accomplish its end. Here it appears to be channeled toward mysterious depths where it seems to disappear entirely.

These depths are the souls emptied of self who are ready to receive scorned love and whose reception Divine Mercy has deigned to accept. The vast shoreless sea takes up its abode there. The Father will never lose His tenderness for His children, and there will always be hearts who love for others, making up the deficiency, until the plan of God's love is realized throughout the universe. This is the subject of . . .

ૐ

The fourth scene: The breadth and the height of the flame make up for the multiplicity of fires.

The majority of people do not realize the capacity of the human heart. A hundred souls whom God has emptied completely can contain the same amount of love as hundreds of millions of others whose limits are a million times less. The Virgin Mary alone gives to God more love than all humanity put together.

The plan of love engendered in the Incarnation and in the Redemption will be realized; nothing will be lacking. The whole river of fire will find an outlet. God, who knows everything in advance, did not send His Son on a useless mission to earth. The request of the Man-God will be fully heard: the will of the Father will be done on earth as it is in Heaven. By love over-flowing in souls, "all will be one as the Father and the Word are one."[32]

Nothing will be lacking. God will be able to say that it is all "very good" indeed.[33]

[32]Cf. John 17:22.
[33]Gen. 1:31.

Descending Fire

د

Let us suppose that a man is building a glorious palace. The magnificence of this structure surpasses anything that we can imagine. The artisans are at work; a body of craftsmen has been summoned; the noise of hammers, saws, and chisels is music to the ears.

While the man attends to his ordinary occupations, and while obligations call him at times to become immersed in work, his soul continues to bask in profound joy. How could he not be happy? While he is here, the work continues; the only thing that really interests him is the construction of the palace.

Then comes the war. Immediately, trowels, levels, and hammers are laid aside. Everyone is at war. Nothing more is done. The walls are half up and waiting to be completed. The man is unconsciously sad; the great work has stopped. It is time lost.

Now victory has sounded and brought joy again to the soul of the builder. The masons and the carpenters resume their work. All is completed. Nothing is left undone.

One day, all will be perfect.

This describes the habitual state of my soul and the sentiments that fill my days: All is completed. One day, all will be perfect. Infinite love, union of the Father and the Son, which tends to communicate itself to the weak and the little, will receive a ready welcome in hearts, will fill and change them into a blazing fire. Do you understand Him who stealthily enters into every niche of our lives, who little by little replenishes from His superabundance the wretchedness of our being, and who will not be stopped until He takes up His dwelling there completely? Oh, sweet music, sweet to the ears and to the heart: All is completed!

During the war of 1914, a lockkeeper secretly unlocked the waters of the Yser over the low-lying plains occupied by enemy troops. The stream crept treacherously over the land, flooding it little by little, and when the enemy noticed it, it was too late. Thousands were swallowed up. Can anyone imagine the satisfaction that man felt when he went home after his bold deed? While he rested easily, all his plans were being executed.

As for myself, is there a thought sweeter than this: "All is completed"? Fire accomplishes its work; the breath of the Lord fills the universe. Yesterday, a violent wind swept through the forest, disturbing each leaf, making each branch groan, and diverting the flight of the bird. Nothing escaped the power of the wind. I thought with emotion, "Look and listen. As on the day of Pentecost, the breath of the Lord fills the world. It wants to invade all of humanity. Offer no resistance; open your heart completely to receive the fiery breath that others refuse. . . . Oh, the unspeakable happiness of feeling oneself so loved!"

The proof of our love must be constantly renewed. It also needs regular nourishment to satisfy its hunger. Where there is no evidence of love, there is indifference.

The proofs of our love and the food that we give it at each moment are the sacrifices that St. Thérèse of Lisieux calls "roses." Our sweet Carmelite sister said all that she had to say on this subject, and so I will limit myself only to what she has written and above all to what she has done.

To specify exactly the kind of roses I must sacrifice to love, it is necessary to remember first the kind of temperament I have and then the providential sacrifices God expects from me.

Descending Fire

The roses I offer consist not in choosing a particular sacrifice but, rather, in confining myself to the present time and place. In contrast with the universality in time and space of my aspirations and my apostolate, my quest for sacrifice will consist especially in loving the present moment and place. I will not pass judgment on them; I will think neither of the past nor of the future; I will live each day my daily bread, and I will repeat interiorly my old short prescription: "Do everything, my God. You will this. . . ." Those are my roses.

I love these two words: *here* and *now*. Of all the moments, past or future, of the whole living universe and all the places in the entire world, the best ones for me are the present moment and the present place, since these are the only things that place me in divine love. I will retain this essential principle: If sometimes, or often, from the depth of my inner solitude I feel the need to throw myself headlong into some activity, I will think of the two words — *here* and *now* — to

which one day God will answer by two opposite expressions: *everywhere* and *always*.

I must live in naked faith and naked hope without light and with no possessions. At every moment,
I must remain as if suspended between earth and
Heaven, clinging to the Father's good pleasure. What
happiness it is to feel that I depend on Divine Mercy
alone, and to be able at each moment to offer God
this total dependence!

So I will reduce myself voluntarily to daily bread,
spiritual as well as material. I will confide the past to
Divine Mercy: God will pardon my offenses as I pardon others. I will throw the past into the bosom of the
Father. The future that I give Him consists of the temp-
tations that, with God's help, I will be able to overcome,
as well as evils of all kinds from which Providence will
deliver me. The last petitions of the Our Father, which
limit me as to the time and place willed by God, answer to the first three petitions, which raise my heart
above time and place into the immensity of God.

Descending Fire

One day, when the Holy Trinity wills it, but above all at the moment of my death, the Holy Trinity will break that double chain which confines me in time and space; and if I have loved Him, my heart will be consumed with the flames of Him who is at the same time both infinite and eternal.

⚜

Recently, I went to my spiritual director, a calm and prudent man, and I said to him, "Father, I am sometimes surprised at my shameless optimism, my boundless confidence, and my utter abandonment. I have the inner conviction that my prayers will be granted, that all will be done according to my expectations, and that God will set no more of a limit on these realizations than I place on abandonment. Tell me truly, Father, am I being overly confident?"

"You are not overly confident. You hope according to the degree that God desires. But you must always add, implicitly at least, 'Whatever God wills.' "

"That is how I understand it, Father."

"Then," he added, "that's good." And he continued, "All that you tell me comes from God. You are
well confirmed in your vocation."

Then, accompanying me to the door, he said,
"Even the holiest people who are thoroughly consis-
tent can have a tendency of this kind."

That is what puts me at ease. I can follow my spiritual instincts. I can give in to the inclinations of my
soul, allow myself to be plunged ever deeper into infinity, forsake the limits of my humanity in order to be
clothed with the Infinite, forget the poor human being
that I am in order to love and be fruitful as God is. . . .
I can break the chains that bind me and allow myself
to disappear into the boundless sea. Oh, the intoxica-
tion of infinite liberty! Oh, the joy and peace of finally
feeling free!

To put any limits on my abandonment would be a
veritable slavery for me. If others have to make great
efforts to boost their confidence, I would have to make
a greater effort to put a bridle on mine. But no, I must

not establish any limit unless it is evident that it is God's will. I have only to allow myself to be carried away by the ardor of my aspirations. Far from stopping me, I must push ever onward. "We obtain from the good God as much as we hope to obtain. . . ."

※

My soul is in a chasm, an abyss without length or breadth, with no measurable depth, in which I feel unfathomable boiling oceans of fire. This life fully satisfies and, at the same time, increases my desires to the point of gnawing at me and consuming me. The more this life borders on the infinite, the more do I thirst to die. I will die one day — perhaps in one year or in thirty years, but I will die.

As far as the eye can see into the shoreless distance, there are glowing flames, and these flames are forever expanding and spreading out.

※

O Father! O Word! O Spirit! Light that shines ever in the mystery of my soul! Voice that speaks to me in secret and without noise of words! Hidden fire that unceasingly consumes me! Hand, sometimes gentle and sometimes firm, that leads me into the shadows! Magnet that draws me without delay.

Jesus: Light, Voice, Fire, Hand, Magnet.

It is a ray of Your light that I see, an echo of Your voice that speaks to me, a spark of Your Spirit that burns me, the driving force of Your hand that guides me, and the attraction of Your call that takes hold of me — without delay, after so many years!

May my spirit see by Your light alone; may my ears be opened to Your voice alone; may my heart burn with Your fire alone. Let me not walk unless my hand is in Yours; let me be helplessly attracted to You. Do everything, since I am capable of nothing.

A covenant with God can change the whole tenor of existence to the point of transforming entirely every aspect of our daily life. When, in darkness, I find myself at a crossroads, it is essential that I choose the right path. Otherwise, each step will take me further away from my intended goal and plunge me deeper into error.

This is all the more true in the supernatural life if it is well understood and well observed.

St. Thérèse of Lisieux one day made a contract. As in all agreements of this kind, she offered a good and she hoped for one in return. What she offered did not give her a strict right to any compensation. She made a free gift, and she begged earnestly for another gift, equally free. This double gift marked the definitive direction of her life in this world and in eternity. In exchange for her gift of herself as victim, she obtained for herself the gift that all the acts of her life would be fused into one single act, the act of God. This is the central idea of her agreement, and this would be henceforth her goal and her reason for existence. St. Thérèse clearly indicates this by these words that introduce her offering of self: "To live in a single act of perfect love . . ."

What way would lead to that life which is a "single act"? The humble Carmelite asks the Father to let flow into her soul the waves of infinite tenderness which are pent up in Him.

This is the tenderness of God Himself.

And it overflows.

And it is God Himself who allows it to overflow.

This tenderness overflows like waves, waves that are contained in God. And they overflow into her soul.

What will become of the soul by this overflowing?

It is made a victim, a victim of holocaust, a victim of holocaust of that love.

And that love is Merciful Love.

After offering herself, St. Thérèse points out the consequences of this offering:

It prepares the victim to appear before God.

She will not have to go to Purgatory.

Finally, it will cast her soul into "the eternal embrace of . . . Merciful Love." Note how well St. Thérèse describes Heaven. For her, Paradise is the eternal embrace of Merciful Love: it is also "love experienced in an eternal face-to-face."

Before the main point of her offering, the saint presents what could be called the preparation: her soul feels its powerlessness. It therefore asks God to be Himself its holiness. Divine holiness will supply for its weakness. Such is the general theme of her preparation.

Now let us look at the details of this preparation: The infinite merits of Jesus belong to the soul who gladly offers them, begging the Father to look at her only through the Face of Jesus and in His Heart burning with love. Her soul also offers all the merits of the saints in Heaven and on earth, their acts of love and those of the holy angels. More particularly, her soul offers the love and the merits of the Blessed Virgin. She looks to Mary and abandons her offering to her. Her soul then asks God to take possession of her and to remain in her as in a tabernacle. She thanks Him for allowing her to pass through the crucible of suffering. She hopes in Heaven to resemble Jesus crucified and to see the wounds of His Passion shining in her glorified body. She desires in the evening of her life to clothe herself with the selfsame justice of the Most High and to receive from His love the eternal possession of Him. She desires no other throne or crown than Jesus Himself.

Divinized and clothed in this manner with divine holiness, her soul knows that God will lift her upward to the summit and that all the acts of her life will

Descending Fire

become the unique act of love that is the life of the Holy Trinity.

How will her soul participate in a human way?

She will do only one thing: she will look for ways to please God. She will not desire to accumulate merits for Heaven; she will desire to work only for love and for the sole purpose of praising the glorious Trinity.

And if, through human weakness, she fails in this participation, she will ask God to supply what is lacking to her. Henceforth, she will ask Jesus to take from her the liberty of displeasing Him. And if, through weakness, she sometimes falls, His divine glance will immediately purify her soul, consuming all her imperfections like fire, which transforms everything into itself.

This Theresian doctrine has universal appeal. It flows from God, from whom she stole its secret, and returns to God after having explored the mysteries of all creation. How can we sum up in a few lines an intelligence so simple that it is inexpressible? For the more perfect something is, the simpler it is; God is simplicity itself.

We can say that there are two principles that dominate Theresian thought: "God is love," and "All is the work of that love."

— The work of that love in the dignity of being children of God.

— The work of that love in the gift of redemption. It is more to prove His love for us that the Father does not permit us to rely on ourselves.

Descending Fire

— The work of that love in our weakness, our powerlessness, which forces us to give, without ceasing, our filial confidence to God alone.

— The work of that love in our fruitless efforts. God requires them, however, because they manifest to Him our loving response. If the Father asks our co-operation in these works, it is with infinite tenderness, because He wants to do nothing without sharing it with His children.

— The work of that love in suffering and death, because these are the things that require the most faith and complete abandonment.

— The work of that love in dryness in prayer, because the silence of God that casts the soul into darkness brings on detachment and a greater purification.

— The work of that love in our work as apostles. Because we are incapable of loving our brethren as we ought, it is God Himself who wishes to love them in us. The tenderness of the Father pours charity into our souls and puts into our hands whatever is needed to feed the sheep who come to us.

— The work of that love in the privilege of the sinner to regain his purity of soul. Divine fire consumes all imperfections and transforms them into itself. St. Mary Magdalene, for example, had been consecrated by divine love, and her heart had become "purer than virgins," as in the song of St. Agnes:[34]

> To love Jesus is already to be chaste.
>
> To touch Jesus is already to be pure.
>
> To receive Jesus is already to be a virgin.

— The work of that love in the happiness of being able to be a martyr without shedding blood — because the fire of charity consumes and can cause death — and in the privilege of appearing before God without passing through Purgatory, because the flames of charity are more purifying than those of Purgatory.

[34]St. Agnes, Roman virgin and martyr.

Descending Fire

In the presence of such excessive paternal tender-
nesses, what must be the attitude of the soul? It has
only to say yes and allow the divine fire to do its work.
Sanctity is above all a disposition of soul. It consists in
abandoning ourselves to the flames of love that overflow from the heart of God, in whose presence man
must hold fast in naked faith. This attitude must be
expressed more in our prayer life than in the apostolic
life. It finds its perfection, beyond the desire to suffer
and to die, in adhering totally to the divine will in
whatever way it is manifested. The essential affinity
between God and man, and the necessary condition
of divine fire finding an outlet in the world, consists in
the all of God and the nothing of man.

To the angel who watched over me at the crossroad of my life, I said, "Enlighten me so that I can advance toward the unknown."

The angel answered, "Walk resolutely in the darkness of naked faith, and, like a child, let yourself be guided by your heavenly Father. Do not ask Him for light, but open your heart to Him, and let the fire of His rejected love flow into you. These flames will become your life, and they will be for you the most splendid of lights. It is love that will make you see in the night."

I dared to question him further: "Angel of the crossroad, how will this fire descend into my soul?"

He said to me, "Contemplate the cascade of fire. It will reveal to you the secret you are looking for."

Descending Fire

☙

My God,
infinite Ocean of tenderness
whose torrents are held back by human malice,
free Your divine desire and permeate
all souls whom You love.

Let us contemplate the summit of the cascade of fire, the Holy Spirit, the mutual love between the Father and the Word, who Himself is God, the God of love and the center of love. The boundless exchange of love that unites the Father and the Son tends to communicate itself and to descend to the one who is the lowest. The more a soul is conscious of its utter weakness and accepts this for love of the Father, the more will the divine fire be inclined to pour itself out on that soul. Such is the flood tide that, at first, fills the vast emptiness.

But this descending fire does not go directly from the Holy Trinity to the soul. The Incarnate Word,

Descending Fire

God and Man, as great as God and as small as man, possesses a Heart that is the sanctuary of charity.

> *Heart of Jesus,*
> *sanctuary of descending love,*
> *pour out, through the opening*
> *of Your wound,*
> *the torrents of Your mercy*
> *on all wretched souls.*

This Heart is the necessary intermediary from which mercy flows. Merciful love, coming from the Trinity, finds its refuge in the Heart of the Man-God; and through the opening made by the lance,[35] torrents of love are poured out upon souls. Through His wounded Heart, God deigns to pour out upon us the treasures of His merciful love. This fire descends only through the sanctuary of the Incarnate Word . . . and through the Immaculate Heart of Mary.

[35] Cf. John 19:34.

"Behold, I stand at the door and knock."[36] This divine fire, passing through the hearts of Jesus and Mary as it descends upon the hearts of all men, finds many closed doors because of the rejection of some and the ignorance of others. Our Lord complains, "I looked for . . . comforters, but I found none."[37]

Yet the flames do not return to their divine Source without response.

This child of the Father opens wide the abyss of her misery and lets the waves of rejected tenderness rush in. This tenderness calls out to all of us: "If anyone thirst, let him come to me and drink."[38] This victim of love, then, stands in the place of the many souls who know how to love and those who do not. In their place, this victim loves with the love with which others should love the heavenly Father.

Hers is a dignified response.

[36]Rev. 3:20.
[37]Ps. 69:20.
[38]John 7:37.

In this way, the flames surrounding the heart of the victim of love return to their Source and their End, the Divine Trinity, with the "breadth and length and height and depth"[39] that respond fully to the loving plan of Redemption. Abundance replaces plenty; the height and breadth of the flame make up for the quantity of fire; the intensity completes what is lacking in extent. In this way, the soul is filled with the fullness of God.

⁕

O infinite movement of love that goes from the Father to the Word and from the Word to the Father, each of whom is a divine Person;

— Limitless flames, which find a proper sanctuary in the Sacred Heart of Jesus and which overflow into the heart of our Mother;

— Rejected or unknown tenderness, which knocks at the door of our hearts and which is refused by many souls, either through weakness or through ignorance;

[39]Cf. Eph. 3:18.

Descending Fire

Do not rise again without a response to the Holy Trinity! Since you are looking for the deepest and widest caverns, flood my heart!

Transform my actions into Yourself, just as the fire changed into fire the entire offering of Elijah, even the dirt, the stones, and the water.[40]

After having thus taken all human misery into Your infinite embrace, return then, in perfect praise to the Divine Trinity, Beginning and End of all things.

Through You, may God receive the fullness of love that He waits for from humanity, and may the Creator's plan be fully realized!

In the ocean of Your love, O divine charity, may the Father's name be hallowed; may His will be done on earth as it is in Heaven!

And may all of mankind be perfected in unity, as the Father and His Incarnate Word are one in You, O Holy Spirit!

[40]Cf. 1 Kings 18:38.

Descending Fire

⚜

Golden Heart of our Mother,
in which the flames that burn
in the Heart of your Son take refuge,
house in our abyss your disdained love,
and then we will love with your full heart.

During the dark hours of the war, I was at my post doing sentry duty. During the alert, while my eyes scanned the stars, awaiting the deadly fire, my heart plumbed the depths of the heavens for another fire, the regenerated fire of Pentecost; and my lips repeated the prayer that, during the last months of her life, Thérèse carried in her heart: "To live in a single act of perfect love . . ." I thought also of the sun at Fatima, which, on October 13, 1917, after having set off a triple display of fireworks, cast over the universe the all-embracing rays of the Holy Trinity as if it wanted to penetrate and consume unreservedly all of humanity and the entire world.

Descending Fire

These encircling rays at Fatima are an appeal and an omen. They have the impetuous movement of the paternal flames that ask to be received and the overflowing of a fire of justice that demands reparation. They give a foretaste of the eternal embrace of Heaven and of the flames that envelop the soul that is damned. This orb that hurled itself on the mountain of Fatima was at the same time a sun of mercy and a sun of justice: a blazing fire that inflames hearts and that ruthlessly destroys with the single purpose of making the Creator loved. These avenging flames are in fact the flames of charity; and Hell has been created out of the Father's tenderness.

Now, out of this burning ardor which is love, Mary dispenses love freely, since she has received it into her Immaculate Heart; and it is in order that we may welcome it that she has us see the other fire, that of anger, which bursts forth from the same sun. She makes me understand that, regardless, the divine fire will consume me — the fire of love or, if I were not her child, the fire of justice, which also has been sparked by the goodness of the Creator.

The scene is a powerful one. It is equally terrible. Another scene, or, rather, a dual scene — by no means frightening but evocative — shows us another aspect of mercy. Fifteen years after showing to a trembling crowd the magnificent sun rushing forward, the Holy Virgin, by two signs that complement each other, showed the scene in which her love stoops to our wretchedness. Our Lady of Beauraing[41] showed her all-radiant heart in the gold of her charity. She whom the Church invokes under the title "House of Gold" desires that the gilded luster of her heart may be the sign of her boundless tenderness.

But the message is still not complete. The solicitude of Mary is a merciful solicitude. Banneux reveals to us the Virgin who leans toward us. Statues that represent her show her clasping her hands to one side in

[41] Beginning in 1932, our Lady appeared to children in Belgium, at Beauraing and Banneux.

order to observe clearly the beseeching attitude of her children.

꙳

When Thérèse was ten years of age, a smile from the Blessed Virgin cured her of a painful affliction. Thérèse's whole life was lit up by that smile. And when death drew near, she wrote, "You who smiled on me in the morning of my life, come, smile on me again, Mother. . . . It is now evening."

Is it not possible that Thérèse wanted to incarnate in herself this smile of the Virgin and to transmit it to humanity? That she wanted to be for us a living smile of Mary? A smile is a little thing, but Mary's smile is the sign of a great interior ardor; it is the tenderness of a Mother who reveals herself through it: "Little child," says Virgil, "from the very beginning, get to know your mother by her smile." The poet continues: "Unhappy is the child whose parents have never smiled."[42]

[42]Virgil, *Eclogues*, no. 4.

But behind the tenderness of Mary, is there not also the tenderness of God, who has revealed Himself to Thérèse?

> *The glance of my God,*
> *His ravishing smile,*
> *that is Heaven for me.*

The heart is a symbol of love, but not a very gracious one, and, besides, it is conventional. The smile is a more refined and more delicate symbol. It is almost ethereal and manifests the loftiest kind of tenderness.

Thus, Thérèse has become, by vocation, a smile: the smile of Mary to humanity. She is, then, not merely a symbol, but the most gracious and most vibrant revelation of that ocean of tenderness that, coming from the Holy Trinity, has passed through the Heart of the Man-God into the heart of Mary and blooms like an immaculate flower on the face of the Virgin.

Descending Fire

✽

O Virgin Mary, whose smile,
while penetrating the soul of
St. Thérèse of the Child Jesus,
gave her to understand your maternal
affection and the love of God our Father,
deign also to smile upon me and to
reveal to me the fragrance of your tenderness.
May a beam of your radiant goodness
penetrate my darkness,
illuminate my whole life,
and place me unreservedly
under your influence. Amen.

❧

Thank you, Ocean of love,
for having subjected my wretchedness
to Your creative fiat
and to Your initiatives alone.

Before constructing the dam at M—, we had to choose a deep valley whose high banks would be able to hold great quantities of water. We also had to find a place with no houses or rich earth, the loss of which would not outweigh the dam's benefits.

After the dam had been constructed, the valley remained what it was. It acquired no richness except a work of architecture whose ordinary beauty did not surpass the stark splendor of the woods descending toward a modest river. It was still an open valley. An essential element changed, however: a lake was formed in its midst, and the abundance of clear water to which it gave asylum poured out its bounty over the distant lands. The valley itself became a lake from which the waters overflowed in a roar.

My soul is that valley. In order for the burning river to be formed there, it must be deep and wide and open to the flow of the rushing stream.

If I had had to drain my valley, I do not believe that I would have had the courage to do it. God has given me the grace to find it empty. He has taken it upon Himself to take away the rich and habitable land. He has hollowed it out deeply and has given me the light to see it and to love my state. He has placed my emptiness directly under the torrent in such a way that I cannot escape from it. If I build a wall to hold back the waters, they will cut a passageway to the side. Paternal love has reduced me to dependence on His initiatives alone.

♪

Thank you, O Father, for having hollowed out the soul of Your child, for having kept it empty. I can do nothing, not even speak to Jesus, without Your special grace. I can only sin, which is non-existence. Thank You, my God, for my being capable of nothing.

I have nothing but shadows and illusions. Every blessing is from You, and You alone are good. Thank You, my God, for letting me have nothing by which I can glorify myself.

My past experience is there to confirm my total incompetence. Every time I wanted to force Your divine will, You were at the turn of the road to remind me of my weakness. I have never been capable of doing anything by myself. I am in blissful dependence at each moment, which makes me count on Your goodwill alone, which compels me to find my joy in my littleness!

It is very sweet to me to recognize my total powerlessness while seeing, in the Person of Your Incarnate Word, Your own humiliations that have communicated their redeeming power to our lowliness.

Descending Fire

Your humiliations are three: the first is "The Word became flesh."[43] The second is the continuation of this: "Christ became obedient unto death, even death on a Cross."[44] And the third crowns the work: "This is my Body. . . . This is the cup of my Blood,"[45] because Your Flesh is true food and Your Blood is true drink.[46] The Word is made flesh. The Word is made flesh and is made obedient unto death on a Cross. Finally, the word this, which, grammatically speaking, does not even convey the gender of a person: "This is the Body of the Word made flesh." Such are the humiliations that permit the creature to open his heart to divine grace and to be prepared to receive it.

༄

My memories of mathematical studies remind me of the Infinite and the finite, which are poles apart. These two meet, however, in those distant regions

[43]John 1:14.
[44]Phil. 2:8.
[45]Cf. Luke 22:19-20.
[46]Cf. John 6:55.

where our spirit scarcely follows. The plenitude of emptiness: the infinitely great and the infinitesimal seek and harmonize with each other. The human soul is, in the sense of emptiness and poverty, what infinite perfection is in the sense of opulence. Extremes meet. Scandal and madness, on account of our ignorance, is the contact point where the secret of the Triune God lies, with weakness of the flesh, with obedience in the face of death, and with the silence of the Eucharist. It is through this that infinite life is poured out upon our wretchedness.

Oh, the happiness of being thus destitute!

If I had much, God would be little in me. If I had less, God would be more in me. If I had little, God would be much in me. If I have nothing, God is all in me.

❧

I do not want to have anything. Thank You, my God, for my poverty.

In my darkness, You are light.

Descending Fire

In my silence, You are voice.
In my wandering, You are the guiding hand.
In the icy emptiness of my soul, You are the lake
of fire.

⚹

Our Lord spoke a few words one day that could be disconcerting to human reasoning: "He who eats my Flesh . . . abides in me, and I in him."[47] Through Holy Communion, Jesus lives in me whole and entire, and my whole being lives in Him. We need not be surprised, then, to hear St. Thérèse say that the divine fire "overflowed into [her] soul," and that at the same time, it "surrounded" her.

Yes, the human heart can take into its depths a divine ardor. It holds that ardor, surrounds it with a dike until its earthly exterior can no longer withstand the assault of the waves dashing it to pieces, and the soul escapes with the flames. At the same time that this

[47]John 6:56.

human heart locks in the torrents, it is surrounded by them; it is overwhelmed by their immensity. It is no longer we who live; it is Jesus with all His love who lives in us.[48]

Is there a grander and more moving spectacle than these flames, which, escaping from the limitless ocean of the Holy Trinity, rush toward our littleness, and after having begged our cooperation, spread out in wide expanses over all creation? My soul, contemplate this mystery, and adore!

Contemplate, first, this infinite circulation of love, which unites the Father to the Word and the Word to the Father, who is the Spirit of the first two Persons and who is God Himself.

Borne upon on this course that, through the Incarnate Word, descends to man's wretchedness, you receive Him and you are surrounded by Him — you and many others. This current flows into your soul and

[48]Cf. Gal. 2:20.

penetrates it; but at the same time it surrounds you.
Empty hearts themselves bring a human element to
the circulation of life of the Holy Trinity: that of
deified humanity through Christ.

With this cooperation of human weakness borne
along the divine current, the circulation of life of the
Three Divine Persons will transform into fire all that
must be transformed in the plan of creation. It will
complete the whole, make up for the deficiency of all,
and render everything perfect until the Father's plans
are accomplished. Thus, all will be one and consum-
mated in unity, as the Father and the Son are one "in
the Holy Spirit."

༈

*I desire, Holy Trinity, that each act of my life might be
stamped with the seal of heroism and martyrdom, that nothing may be lost in each of the moments given to me through
Your generosity. I desire to thank You, to beseech You, to love
You without intermission, and to bring about in a perfect
manner the cooperation You expect from Your creatures.*

Alas! Reality is different. My times of emptiness are numerous, at least in appearance, when I hardly am permitted to think about You, when my physical capacity is inadequate for intellectual learning, when it seems that I have done nothing. I have done nothing, and so I must be resigned to wait for better days.

Better days? But these empty days are the best. They are really empty only in appearance. That is when You force me to put my finger on the reality of what I am and so make me experience my complete powerlessness. Happy days are those empty days, in which You fill me with Yourself, in which You teach me secretly, consume me, and strengthen me; in which You allow Your light, Your love, and Your power to pierce my soul.

It is in these times of silence when, without words, You speak to me of everything: about the total accomplishment of the plan of creation, Incarnation, and Redemption; about the whole Mystical Body of the Incarnate Word; about the sanctifying work of the Holy Spirit; about Your fruitfulness, O Father.

Descending Fire

It is then that You make me understand the richness of the present hour. Each of these moments gives me a share in the unlimited treasure of Your mercy. Each moment is a new discovery for me, a personal gift of Your tenderness. Like a beautiful gold-piece, this gift bears the imprint of descending flames on its front; and on its back there is a smooth surface on which the human response will be engraved.

May you be blessed, God of merciful love, for the days on which I have done nothing. These totally powerless days have the potential to become days of unlimited power.

Death! My great friend!

I love life with all of my being. I enjoy intensely all that life has to offer: the beauty of nature, the harmony of sounds, intellectual pleasures, the joys of society. All that the Creator gives me is a source of delight for me.

Yet, death is my friend: a fleshless, cold, silent friend, fearful to me. But a friend — and even my great friend.

Since Christ has sacrificed Himself, death has become life. That is why I love it. Like the winter's snow, it protects the dormant seed: "Unless a grain of wheat falls into the earth and dies, it remains alone; but if it dies, it bears much fruit."[49] In reality, "life is changed,

[49]John 12:24.

83

not ended."[50] Christ will change the form of our piti-
able bodies and will give us glorious bodies.[51] But God
has placed one condition on our transformation: that
we accept our wretchedness. And as death is the
supreme affliction, it is also the supreme grace.

On that day, when my eyes grow dull, when I am no
longer able to raise my arms, when my lips are silent,
when my mind is incapable of thought, and when my
heart feels the chill of death; on that day, when I am
no longer able to count on any creature, when I
know that I am alone in the presence of God with
nothing that can distract me; on that day of extreme
nakedness, if I have accepted and loved it beforehand,
God can in an instant pour into my soul more love
than my efforts, aided by grace, would have been able
to acquire in hundreds of years. That miracle will be
performed.

[50]Preface, Mass for the Dead.
[51]Cf. Phil. 3:20-21.

In one second, the Infinite will fill the almost end-less caverns of my miserable soul with a flame that will shatter my earthly exterior. The great wave will con-sume all that remains of my humanity, and I will die of love. I will die a martyr of this love after having been freed by its transforming action. I will be love, and it is God who will do it all. He will do it all at the mo-ment when humiliation has reached its depth, when it is clearest that I can attribute nothing to myself, and when I am tempted to cry out with Christ, "My God, my God, why hast Thou forsaken me?"[52]

My death will have been ennobled by that of Jesus; my lowliness will have been purified by that of Jesus; my transformation will have been effected through communication of the glory of Jesus glorified.

Death, my somber friend!

The death of my neighbor, the death of all those whom the Word Incarnate calls to His glory must also

---

[52]Mark 15:34.

be the moment of their transformation. For the majority of souls, death is a surprise. To what extent are they prepared? A parish priest often asks this question with anxiety. Just as they will be at the moment when the soul leaves the body, so they will be for all eternity. What I must do, then, is ask God to ensure that their lamps be well lit at the moment of their departure.

In the Mystical Body of Christ, the Communion of Saints can make up for what is lacking in those souls at the point of death. If God wishes, a single ray of His light, one spark of His love, poured into the soul at this decisive moment can call forth a glow sufficient to blot out every blemish. If God wishes — it depends on His will. Our role, then, is to love our lowliness, to unite it to the incarnate and crucified Word in order that His love might perfectly supply what is lacking to these souls, whatever may be the time or place in which they live, are living, may have lived, or ought to live.

For each soul, as for me, death must be the friend, the great friend.

❀

My God, I beg of You, by Your unspeakable humiliations, when the moment of the last trial comes to each of Your predestined ones, pour out upon them enough ardor to enable them to love You for all eternity in the measure that You expect of them.

In this manner, Your plan will be realized in them. In this manner, the Mystical Body of Jesus will be complete. Nothing will be lacking in it.

✳

At the foot of the cascade near Interlaken: from a distance it looks as if a sash of muslin is softly caressing the rugged mountain. Reality is different: the stream rushes forth with a thunderous noise, falling from rock to rock, collapsing into a fissure, only to be divided with greater force and crash at the bottom in millions of drops that lash at our face and make us shudder. The water does not fall quietly into the depths like a crystalline brook. The flood overflows, surging over large rocks that block its course, and seeks to spread itself far and wide before continuing on its way.

The cascade of fire — it, too, works to widen. Having touched the lowliness of our being, it seeks to spread itself toward other souls in the distance. The second commandment is like unto the first, says the Lord.[53] The flames, which must return to God, must pass first through other souls and, in turn, transform them into a torrent of fire.

Let us consider for the moment the movement that carries the embraced soul toward other souls in which it sees the beloved God; this is the fundamental tendency of the fiery cascade to grow wider and wider. The tide no longer descends; yet it does not rise; it stretches out toward all those who resemble us. But it is the same tide that has descended, that will rise, and that extends itself far and wide.

St. Thérèse of Lisieux put it this way: "Never," she said to Jesus, "will I reach the point of loving my Sisters as You have loved them if You do not love them in me." She wrote in the same vein, "When I am charitable, it is Jesus who is acting in me; the

---

[53] Cf. Matt. 22:38-39.

more I am united to Him, the more also do I love
all my Sisters." The love that, coming from the Holy
Trinity, invades our wretchedness is consequently the
same love that is carried to human creatures. Our soul
loves the Creator and our neighbor with a love that
is not our own but is the life of the Three Divine
Persons.

So, it is not difficult to explain the boundless affection Jesus asks of us Christians in regard to our neighbor. Is it possible for us to "love one another as Jesus
has loved us"[54] unless by the Spirit of Love? We likewise
understand better, up to this point, that Jesus wants
to see unity between Christians. How many different
creatures, separated by time and space, can be perfected in unity without the bond of unique charity?

✤

I have contemplated the cascade of fire in its general effect. Such a boundless landscape will appear in

[54]Cf. John 13:24.

Descending Fire

its immense size before the eye can discern the details. I have followed the movement of the living flames — at first in the bosom of the Holy Trinity, then in the two sanctuaries of Jesus and Mary.

I heard the loud clash of doors being closed against the persistence of the divine fire that wants to pierce souls. Then, after having tried to offer my extreme wretchedness in reparation, I received in me the river of fire. I see the flood now reaching out far and wide toward my neighbor so it may rise again, enriched by human cooperation, toward the One who is the Beginning and the End, the Alpha and the Omega.[55]

And all of this fire is the same as the tongues of fire that came down at Pentecost and "filled the whole house,"[56] which is the Church. This burning will continue until the end of time. Like a powerful wind that

[55] Cf. Rev. 21:6.
[56] Cf. Acts 2:3.

shakes the depths of the forest, "the breath of God fills the whole universe":

> *Our Father in Heaven,*
> *and you, Mother of God and our Mother,*
> *fill with the spirit of love*
> *Your whole house,*
> *limitless in time and space.*

*

Jesus, Mary, fill my hand
with the food that You
reserve for Your sheep.
and without leaving Your arms,
without turning my head,
I will give to each one what You wish.

Jesus, make me delight in preaching in
the desert, in seeing fruits fall before they are ripe,
in perceiving in them the air of death,
since they bear within themselves
the mystery of love.

We do not always live in Heaven, nor even between Heaven and earth. Direct contact with souls

occupies a notable part of our life. What must be our attitude toward those who are entrusted to us?

The answer to this question is given to us again by the saint of Lisieux. One day when she had care of the novices, she wrote, "I judged at first glance that the task was beyond my strength. So, placing myself very quickly into the arms of God, I said, 'Lord, I am too little to nourish Your children. If You want to give them, through me, what is fitting to each one, fill my little hand; and without leaving Your arms, without even turning my head, I will give Your treasures to the soul who will come asking me for nourishment.' "

This solution to the problem is ingenious and perfect. It is God who fills the hand of the apostle. We must not leave the arms of the Father, nor even turn away from contemplation of Him. The treasures that we distribute will be those of Jesus, and it is our soul itself that should ask for them.

So, while the universe is in turmoil, the child remains close to his father, and lets the riches of the fire that God allows to pass through her hands flow into receptive hearts.

Apostolic action does not diminish contemplation; it completes it. It is not obliged to "leave God for God," according to a popular expression. It draws us into closer union with the God of Heaven, while allowing Him to act in us with respect to our neighbor, in whom we see God.

But we obtain this favor only by humiliation accepted with love and gratitude.

St. John the Baptist prepared the way for Christ while preaching in the desert. The desert is unproductive sand. It has also the searing wind that set afire all the forerunners of the Old Testament. The desert is unproductive because it is burning. Its fiery breath hinders it from producing.

Unhappy is the apostle who complacently counts the results obtained by his own efforts. It is true that we must not reproach him too quickly. To be sure, who is not exposed to giving himself credit for his successes? But the love of the Father has found a preventive remedy against such illusions. This remedy is apparent failure, above all when it is continuous. Constant humiliation is one of the greatest graces that can win for us divine love, provided we accept it with a childlike heart and that we use every opportunity that Providence offers.

St. Thérèse liked "to see fruits fall before they are ripe." In the spiritual domain, the air of death of damaged fruit bears within itself the mystery of love. As children of the Father, the more we taste the bittersweetness of an apparently unsuccessful work, the more the divine fire quickens our soul and works in us what our weakness cannot accomplish.

If I were to make a trip around the world in spirit, traveling from the burning lands of the equator to the white silence of Alaska, from the unexplored forests of Brazil to the bustle of New York and Moscow, and if, going back then over the course of the past centuries, I were to consider our own ancestors and the highly civilized Greeks, and the slaves who built the pyramids, I would see evidence of an inescapable, unforgiving law — the law of suffering: "The whole creation has been groaning in travail together until now,"[57] writes St. Paul.

He continues, "Not only the creation, but we ourselves, who have the first fruits of the Spirit, groan

[57]Rom. 8:22.

inwardly as we wait for adoption as sons, the redemption of our bodies."[58] These groanings are readily understood by God's children. They are a preparation for
the resurrection of our bodies. When suffering is accepted well and offered up, it produces this marvel.

The great problem with trial is that the vast majority of mankind does not accept suffering willingly.
Even in Christian countries, how many people in
times of grief, or sickness, or difficulty adopt an attitude of submission to the divine will? More often
they take a fatalistic approach in one form or another
rather than the humble and simple acceptance of suffering. What, then, can we say of those who do not
know Christ or who live as if they do not know Him?

Such groaning cannot be considered an acciden-
tal aspect of human existence; its persistence, since
the dreadful sentence in the garden of Paradise, has
made it a law that is applied to all the details of our

[58]Rom. 8:23.

life. Will divine Wisdom allow this groaning to be wasted?

God does not want anything to be wasted. Not one drop of the divine Blood poured out on Calvary will remain ineffective. Not one drop of human blood should remain unproductive. The love of God, which has been poured into our hearts by the Holy Spirit,[59] will be the soul of all suffering. If God accepts our prayer, we can introduce into every trial one spark of the spiritual flame that is in us and so make of it an act of love.

"Lord," wrote St. Gertrude, "I desire to draw into my heart, by my fervent desires, all the afflictions and fears, the sorrows and the anguish that no creature has ever been able to endure, not for the glory of the creature but for the faults arising out of its own weakness. I offer all of that to You as a high-priced myrrh."[60]

[59] Cf. Rom. 5:5.

[60] From the prayers of St. Mechtilde and of St. Gertrude, Maredsous Abbey, "Prayer on the Day of the

Descending Fire

Within the human heart, divine charity can make up for what is lacking in the sufferings of the world, because fire transforms everything into itself.

In my childlike heart, I will carefully gather all the incomplete trials of the entire world, those of all peoples, all races, and all times, and will make them my own. I will let none be wasted. The ardor of the flames to which my poverty has given refuge will melt all these inadequate works and will separate the pure metal from the dross.

❧

The sufferings of humanity will return to You, O my God. They will be offered to You purified and made conformed to the sorrows that the Man-God endured on earth. Nothing will be fruitless. Moreover, each trial that Your goodness has permitted in the universe will become one more flame of love for You, Father.

Epiphany." St. Gertrude (1256-c. 1302), German mystic.

✸

May You be loved, O my God, in every suffering;
let Your tenderness poured out upon us be the soul of all
suffering!

May You be loved in the tears at birth and in those
of infancy; in the growing pains of adolescence and in the
anxieties of mature age!

May You be loved in the chill of poverty and old age;
in the sorrows of separation and the weariness of exile!

May You be loved in sickness of body and of soul; in
those of individuals and of nations!

May You be loved in the horrors of war and of fam-
ine; in all the tears of the present and of those yet to
come!

May You be loved in the groaning of creatures de-
prived of reason; in the destruction of animals, of vegeta-
tion, and of minerals!

May You be loved, O my God, in every suffering;
let Your tenderness poured out upon us be the soul of all
suffering!

Descending Fire

May You be loved, O my God, in every death; let Your tenderness poured out upon us be the light and the flame of all death!

May You be loved in the final hour of distress and the last hour of suffering that paves the way for the final infusion of Your love!

May You be loved in the death of those who love You too little or whose heart is not pure enough!

May You be loved by the ray of dawn that You will send them, which, in a single instant, can make ready the eternal vision!

May You be loved by the spark that You will communicate to them and that, in one second, can set the soul afire for all eternity!

May You be loved in the grain of wheat that dies before it bears fruit and in the man who undergoes ruin with the hope of revival!

May You be loved, my God, in every imperfect act; let Your tenderness poured out upon us be the perfection of every imperfect act!

May You be loved in every work performed without sufficient good intentions or lacking an adequate degree of charity!

May You be loved in too many half-hearted sacrifices, in too many lifeless prayers, in too few generous efforts!

May You be loved in vain words and useless thoughts, in self-centered affabilities and in the truths that touch on falsehood!

May You be loved by Your light that transforms by Your consuming flame!

May You be loved, O my God, in all that does not have the intelligence to comprehend You or the will to love You; let Your tenderness poured out upon us be the voice of every irrational creature!

May You be loved in the nightingale who sings to You without knowing it and in the bee who whispers Your name without knowing it!

May You be loved, divine Beauty, in the rose; and You, strength of the Almighty, in the sturdy oak!

Descending Fire

May You be loved, my God, in the powerful and terrible ocean and in the cliff that stops the flood!

May You be loved in the land that bears us, in the wind that caresses us, in the forest that calls us!

May You be loved in shadow, which throws light into relief; and in the cold, which bears witness to fire!

⚜

Imagine a man who has committed the worst faults: his past, which pleads wretchedness and makes him tremble at the thought of divine judgment, is always before him. Sometimes in moments of solitude, he is tempted to say with Judas, "My sin is too great."

But here is what God reveals to this sinner. The stream of fire that comes down from Heaven can cleanse (since it is a stream) and can consume (since it is fire) all the blemishes accumulated by this sinner. Better still, these devouring flames can change the wretchedness of his life into so many acts of love.

How can such a transformation take place? The nature of this divine fire solves the mystery. It is a fire that descends, a merciful fire. It seeks out the lowest. It ignores the summit, even the shady places situated halfway up the mountain. It abases itself and descends toward misery. This is its nature.

And what does this merciful love accomplish in wretched souls? It is not looking simply for a refuge, like an outcast in quest of shelter. This divine fire is at work. Like material fire that transforms all things into itself, this torrent of infinite tenderness cleanses and purifies the wretchedness of the one who recognizes it and accepts it as would a child. Moreover, it can transform the failures of our frail nature into divine charity.

But what really is this torrent of descending fire? It is the reciprocal love of the Three Divine Persons; it is the life of God. The Holy Trinity Itself comes to us and communicates to us what It is. When the Word espoused His sacred humanity on the day of the Incarnation, He called to espousal all creatures who would one day assume human nature and who would allow His ineffable love to act.

Descending Fire

Is not the sinner, then, excluded from this call of the Incarnate Word? Not only is he not excluded, but it is to him particularly that the tenderness of Jesus reaches out, provided that he entrusts himself to love just as the child entrusts himself to the goodwill of his parents. Our Lord came to call not the just, but sinners.[61]

꙼

Does the divine flame that is received into the sinful soul limit its action to the one who has received it? Certainly not. Many hearts close the door on the One who knocks! Man, in his wretchedness, can open himself to the assault of that love rejected by others. He can give sanctuary to that charity scorned by his brothers and expand his heart to the size of God.

What will the consequence of this assault be? This weak child of the Father will love the Creator in a manner worthy of His tenderness. With the love that

[61] Cf. Matt. 9:13.

is the life of the Holy Trinity, he will love in place
of those who have refused these flames; he will love
with that charity that has been offered to them and
that they have not accepted. Placed in the heart of
the Church, then, he will render an affection equal
to what the eternal God looks for in the plan of creation, Incarnation, and Redemption.

❧

In the heart of Your child,
O Father, stir up only flames,
for the sake of the whole Mystical Body.

    Why, my God, why, amid life's obstacles always and
from every side, from each flower to each thorn in the
path — why has a twofold mysterious assurance guided
my earthly voyage without wavering? From the beginning
there has been a light, dwelling I know not where; sometimes a glimmer or a soft light, at other times a dazzling
beacon — but always pure and alive — a light that continuously transforms into itself all that I have and all that
I am. Moreover, at times hidden under the ashes and at
times an immense conflagration, there has also been a fire

Descending Fire

*that consumes and transforms into fire the most intimate
fibers of my being.*

Why?

*Why is this radiant passion limitless in time and space,
universal and perpetual; as extensive as the Mystical Body
and as durable as divine love? At every period and every
turn of my life from the age of ten until, as a man, I witnessed the fulfillment of my childhood yearnings, why has
there been so evident in my soul this spiritual river of fire
as if it flowed from a volcano? Why this mystery? Why this
ultimate assurance at every moment that all will be accomplished one day, perhaps only in death and totally without
restriction, an assurance that has never left me even under
the most difficult circumstances?*

Why, why?

*Why do You have the patience and the perseverance to
sustain in my soul this light, despite the ceaseless obstacles
that my human weakness creates? My soul's resistance seems
like defiance of Your infinite mercy, which tends to descend
to what is most unworthy. Yet You do not grow weary.*

Why all these mysteries, O my God?

I see only one answer. You give it in the holy Gospel: Your "breath" moves where it wills. We do not know where it comes from or where it goes.[62] Where does the wind come from? What course does it take? We do not see it passing by. We only feel its action. It is in this manner, O Holy Trinity, that Your divine breath operates in our hearts.

To this movement of Your Spirit, O my God, I will respond only by a prayer.

This desire has become the sentiment of my soul which is identified with my thoughts and my life. It is a transformation of my being into Your flame, O Spirit of the Father and of the Son: fire of the Mystical Body of Christ.

Here is my desire, my sole desire. I live for it; I will die for it. I will live for it through all eternity. It pursues me during the day and illuminates my night. It is my nourishment, my health, my passion, and my immense happiness:

[62] Cf. John 3:8.

Descending Fire

To give myself credit for nothing, to feel my total incompetence, to possess nothing as mine; and in proportion to this voluntary and acknowledged weakness, to be totally bound to live Your life, to be abandoned unreservedly to the One who is eternal — to my Father, who loves me beyond all measure, and to the Holy Trinity, who burns to make me participate in Its divine life; to be totally bound to wait for the One who possesses all and who desires to give all. What unspeakable joy!

I know it. I feel it. Your fire, O my God, surrounds me, pierces me through, insinuates its way into the most intimate fibers of my heart, fills to overflowing the almost infinite caverns of my soul, and responds to my littleness by making me a participant of Your divinity.

My lips speak of daily events; my eyes behold houses and trees; my ears hear conversations. But in all of this my heart sees only shadows and illusions. You alone, adorable Trinity, are the reality.

*It is You whom I seek; it is You for whom I thirst.
Toward You alone my lips, my eyes, my hands,
and my ears aspire.*

*My will no longer loves nor desires anything in
itself. Another fire burns it — a fire that gives to all
life its reason for being and brings joy to my heart.
It loves through Your love, adorable Trinity, through
the Spirit that proceeds from the Father and from the
Son. My will has become this love; it is lost in the
divine fire like wood or gold that is transformed into
fire.*

*My desire is the accomplishment of this transfor-
mation. But that is not all. My humble prayer will
be complete only if it reaches out to these expanding
flames. Divine Creator, Your work of love comes
so fresh from Your paternal hands — O unsullied
mornings, daily dawns, annual springtime, perpetual childhood of life! Your untainted works have
been damaged by the first sin, Original Sin. The
Redemption, with the sanctifying action of Your*

Descending Fire

Spirit, has more than restored the work of creation.
But You expect the cooperation of the creature.
Man must complete what is lacking to the Passion
of Christ; he must grow in Jesus until he is a perfect
man.[63] He has His part to play in the accomplishment of the life-giving circulation of flames that,
emanating from Your adorable Trinity, must unite
the Mystical Body of Christ in the very perfection
of unity.

Spread yourself out, divine flames; raise up a
great number of perfectly empty chasms fit to receive
you and ready to be consumed to the very end.

My God, in Your ardor, inflame every human
act in the entire universe that lacks the right inten-
tion or pure charity. Pass the suffering of all humanity, past, present and future, through the flame.
Enlighten and enkindle the hearts of the dying; give
to them the ray of light and the spark of love that

[63]Cf. Col. 1:24; Eph. 4:13.

116

will prepare them for eternity. To creatures deprived of reason, to the birds and the trees, to the seas and the mountains, to grass and insects, give a song that extols Your love through the voice and the heart of man. Of all that Your paternal tenderness has created, may nothing be forgotten. May all be perfect in creation. In creation, sanctify Your name, establish Your reign, and accomplish Your will.

This is, Holy Trinity, my fervent supplication.

✻

My God,

who has permitted these times of persecution,
let the intensity of love replace its vast expanse,
the height of the flame replace the number of fires,
and make its burning heat equal to the
perilous dangers of the entire world.

The Holy Spirit acts in a different manner according to the various periods in the history of the Church. He keeps watch over the needs of the moment.

It is hardly necessary to say what the actual needs of the Church are. The Christian world has grown smaller since the war. To the great number of those who ignore the Gospel or have left the Church in troubled times we must add entire nations whose faith is uprooted by war and whom war threatens to plunge headlong into frightening materialism. It is to them, above all, that our thoughts go out. It is their bondage that is the principal concern of the Catholic soul. Must we simply be resigned to bow our head and, while waiting for better days, bear the loss of a considerable part of humanity? Since when would the head of an army have the right to limit the number of souls he would save? Did Christ not die for all men? Despite ignorance and destitution, must we not give to God all the love He expects from the universe and complete what is lacking in Christ's Passion?

But how can we make up for so many deficiencies? There is so much to repair; there are so few workers! There are so few saviors to obtain so many results! So few for so many!

We must face it. It seems the problem cannot be solved.

But this is what the Spirit says:

*Intensity can make up for size; a few, for a great
number; a minority, for a lukewarm majority. Cannot
the ocean outweigh a thousand rivers; the star outweigh a
profusion of lamps and domestic fires; the storm outweigh
all human strength? Moreover, the Incarnate Word surpasses our intelligence, the Holy Spirit transcends the human heart, and the paternity of the Father is beyond all
fruitfulness.*

This is what the Spirit says:

*Early in the atomic era, man penetrated the very heart
of matter and now handles like an unconscious child the
terrible reserves of energy hidden in the core of the atom;
in this new epoch, when humanity, entangled in its pride,
has received from the Creator the frightening privilege of
scrutinizing the depths of matter and risks destroying itself
through the use of this science; in this critical period, when
mankind seeks a greater soul and the mechanistic side of
man demands a mystical part, the merciful love of God is
willing to enlarge the heart of man in proportion as man
has attained power over material things. The soul of this*

humanity, transformed by the divine flames, must be enlarged to fit the dimensions of its immense body, and those that materialism has led astray can, if God wills it, receive the effects of this fire without limit. The pillars of fire must rise again to God higher and stronger even as they are less numerous. These pillars of fire can also, to the extent that God wills, be given to those whom materialism attacks on all sides and who will probably be overwhelmed by it one day.

Matter will not kill the spirit.

*

Animals, vegetables, minerals, creatures of love
who, on the day when the Word assumed
a material body, were called to become
a hymn of pure fire, sing perfectly the
love of the Creator, by the voice and
the heart of man united to Christ.

This afternoon, I came down the road from P—,
a splendor of color. Shining coins from the sun were
scattered among the somber fiery hues of the foliage.
I did not dare to move. The love of the Creator lay
hidden behind each leaf and ran mysteriously through
each leaping of the brook. I did not dare to make a
sound, O Father, in order not to disturb Your flame,

which could be divined in this forest fire. On the
crest, the trees seemed like so many burning bushes
that were, like that of Moses, "burning, yet . . . not
consumed."[64]

And I thought of all the greenery in the universe,
of the tender shoots of spring, of the mighty foliage of
summer, of the fiery display in autumn. The Father has
a hand in all of it, even in places where man has never
been. Throughout the millennia, delicate plants have
enriched great unexplored regions of America and
Oceania without one human creature having ever
been able to contemplate them or to extol them. Has
God, then, covered in vain so many unknown lands
with the most exquisite carpets that rains or cold can
quickly return to dust?

What about, in those same unexplored regions, the
choruses man has not heard: songs of the birds, harmo-
nies of the forests, the joy of the plaintive or howling

[64]Exod. 3:2.

winds that blow through the branches, the crystal-clear murmurs of the springs, the eternal roaring of the ocean? From there it spreads out to all forms of life in lands unexplored. The Church sings of them in the *Benedicite* Canticle: all the showers and the dew; the winds which are breath of God; the fires and the flames, the frosts and the heat; the ice, the snow, and the frozen blossoms; light and darkness, the lightning that strikes the rock, and all the flashes of lightning; the clouds that are hidden in the hollows of the mountains, all the mountains and all the hills; the hidden fountain and the secluded rivers.[65] And the same question rises again to my lips: Has divine Wisdom freely given so much beauty in vain — beauties that will disappear without having been witnessed by anyone with a rational soul?

But the tenderness of the Father has foreseen all. Nothing that He has made will be useless and lacking

[65] Cf. Dan. 3:57-66.

a response. What the eye does not see, the heart divines. The tree, the flower, the grass, all that grows, as well as the invisible rock and the star whose brilliance the telescope could never perceive: these are the work of His love and find their whole reason for being in the tenderness that man renders to them through Christ. Divine charity poured into our heart must serve as the song of creatures who do not have rational souls. That will be the complement to what is lacking. It is God who, with our heart, will draw from every work of His hands the measure of love He expects from them.

When the Word came down to earth, He did not take a soul only; He united His soul with a body made of flesh and bone. From that time, inanimate matter, which God had already found "very good" after the creation and which had been cursed after Adam's sin, was found to be completely rehabilitated and even raised to a greater stature. In uniting to His divine Person a body drawn from the earth, as ours is, the

Word made man exalted all matter. St. Francis of
Assisi had reason to say that, on Christmas night,
we should give the animals extra food. By the Incarnation, the animal, the vegetable, and the mineral took
up their part in creation's song. In a mysterious language that the voice and heart of man must express,
they sang the glory and love of the Creator, of the
Man-God, and of Mary, the most perfect of all
creatures.

But what can the human heart do if it is not filled
with divine fire?

Sing then, O child of God! Sing for the love of
your Father. Sing, O leaf, all the leaves of the world.
Sing, O star, all the stars. Give to them a language, a
language of love that ascends in a hymn of pure flame
to the heart of the One who creates all things.

Since 1920, for entire days I sometimes whisper ceaselessly, "Inflame my heart with the fire that consumed all the angels and saints together." I did not know how such a thing could be possible, but I was not concerned about it. Eventually, the following words were added: "and which must inflame all souls." The love that animates the saints is love graciously received; rejected love is the love that souls should have received.

Since 1920, I have also caught myself repeating thousands of times, "May my heart be an infinite furnace," or "May my heart love You with all of *Your* love." I did not know how this could happen, but I felt that it would be so. These are expressions of a unique

tendency whose depth I have not always been able
to measure and which finds its accomplishment in the
invasion of the flames of Merciful Love.

At times, I pray this way:

> *Through Your efficacious grace,*
> *by which we possess both the will and the act,*
> *grant to my wretched soul and to*
> *all the souls You have predestined*
> *the degree of perfection and love You have*
> *established in Your eternal plan.*

I do not know of a more appeasing prayer. It satisfies the soul completely and without reservation places
it in union with His divine will. It leaves to efficacious
grace the unlimited power of His action.

At other times, the thought of the universal Church
attracts me to St. Catherine of Siena,[66] and I say to
her, "St. Catherine of Siena, you who have borne on

---

[66] St. Catherine of Siena (c. 1347-1380), Dominican
tertiary.

your shoulders the vessel of Holy Church and all the sins of her members, you whom God has accepted as a victim offered to His justice for the Catholic Church, grant that in favor of this same Church, God will welcome many souls and accept my childlike weakness as a victim offered to His merciful love."

Still, at other times, my spirit turns to the angels, my brothers, and my friends, and we renew this exchange:

Angels of God,
pure lights and pure flames,
give to my wretchedness the ardor of your love,
and since you do not have the privilege of suffering,
take in exchange my trials and my death.

A prayer that summarizes it all is the following:

Holy Trinity,
pour into my poverty Your merciful love.
Make of me the victim and the martyr of Your flames,

Descending Fire

> *and purify me by their action.*
> *Leave in me only fire —*
> *Your fire, O lovable Trinity.*
> *Transform my acts,*
> *and make of them a single perfect act.*
> *Expand this perfect act, which is Your act.*
> *May it be the totality of all the misery*
> *You desire to set afire by Your flames.*

All is accomplished.

During the hours in which I see and am moved under the influence of these words, my soul is left to swing to and fro at the mercy of the breeze of the divine Spirit. It is carried along by abandonment.

＊

Our tumultuous era is too often indifferent to the great drama whose theater is the entire universe.

— The drama that puts face-to-face the Creator and His creatures, Heaven and earth, spirit and matter, light and darkness, love and hate.

— The drama whose prize is itself the purpose of creation and the whole work of the Incarnation and the Redemption.

— The drama that was begun by the revolt of Lucifer and his followers and which continued on earth, near the tree of the earthly paradise, and which lasted until the arrival of the Messiah.

— The drama that, according to the testimony of the seer of Patmos and of St. Paul, continues in the combat of the "saints" against the heresy of the Beast[67] and against the "mystery of iniquity."[68]

— The drama that sees the "son of perdition" rise up against everything that is called God, take his seat in the temple of God, and display all the seduction of iniquity for those who are lost, because they did not open their heart to love the truth.[69]

— The drama that alone can explain the terrible events of the present time, and which the Incarnate Word will one day resolve by exterminating the Beast by the breath of His mouth,[70] by the breath of love that unites Him to the Father.

This struggle to the death has as its purpose the fire of divine love, which desires to descend into souls who try to hold back the power of darkness.

[67]Cf. Rev. 13. The seer of Patmos is St. John the Evangelist, who was exiled on the island of Patmos when he wrote the Book of Revelation.

[68]Cf. 2 Thess. 2:7.

[69]Cf. 2 Thess. 2:3-4, 10.

[70]Cf. 2 Thess. 2:8.

⚜

Contemplate, O my soul, this immense current that unites the Father to His Word and the Word to His Father, and who is one Person.

This infinite inferno is enough to bring about the happiness of the Blessed Trinity. But the love of God tends to communicate itself, and, as outside of God, nothing exists that can equal Him, this love tends to descend.

Contemplate this cascade, which, like a ribbon of fire, descends on the whole of creation.

— This cascade, which finds in the Sacred Heart of the Man-God a perfect sanctuary, but desires to diffuse itself more widely.

— This cascade, which shelters in a second sanctuary, the Immaculate Heart of Mary, but tends to continue its pursuit toward humanity.

— This cascade, which knocks at the door of all hearts and, too often, crashes against the barriers set up by the Beast.

Descending Fire

— This cascade, which searches out chasms to fill them entirely, to hide there its rejected waters, and to defeat the "son of perdition."

✢

This cascade will continue to descend until the Spirit prevails over matter, light over darkness, and the mystery of fire over the mystery of iniquity.

— Until the work of the six days of creation is completed and God sees that all is very good.

— Until the Father finds in His children all the love He expected from them at the time of the coming of the Light hidden under the form of flesh.

— Until the work is complete of the divine fire that Jesus came to kindle on earth and which He desires to see burning.[71]

[71]Cf. Luke 12:49.

Prayers

❧

Prayer for the Unique Act
Holy Trinity,
whose life is a unique and infinite act,
may all the acts of my life be a single act,
Your unique and eternal act of reciprocal love,
and may I thus live in a single act of perfect love.

❧

Prayer for One Love
May one love, that which consumes You,
Father, Son, and Holy Spirit,
that which inflames the hearts of
Jesus, Mary, and the saints,
also inflame the heart of Your child
and all the souls whom You desire to save.

Descending Fire

Prayer to the Sacred Heart of Jesus
Heart of Jesus, sanctuary of descending love,
pour out, through the opening of Your wound,
the torrents of Your mercy
on all wretched souls.

❧

Prayer to Christ on the Cross
Jesus on the Cross, allow me to gather up
all the Blood that You lost
for all the souls for whom You
burned with thirst on Calvary,
and allow me to gather up
all Your rejected love for all those You
loved from the height of the Cross.

❧

Prayer to the Heart of Mary
Golden Heart of our Mother,
in which the flames that burn

in the Heart of your Son take refuge,
house in our abyss your disdained love,
and then we will love with your full heart.

⚜

Prayer to the Immaculate
Mary, most pure mirror of the
Word veiled in the flesh,
brightness of the Glory that came
down to earth, accustom my eyes to the
light of love, so that in you I may see Jesus
and, in Jesus, the Father.

⚜

Prayer to the Word Who
Has Assumed Our Nature
Incarnate Word, who has willed to assume
our nature in order to raise to divinity
whoever has a human nature, grant
that all mankind may be consumed in unity,
as You Yourself are one with the Father.

Descending Fire

❧

For the Liberation of Divine Desire
My God,
infinite Ocean of tenderness,
whose torrents are held back by human malice,
free Your divine desire and permeate
all the souls whom You love.

❧

Prayer for Human Participation
in the Divine Plan
Perfect God who,
in Your infinite discretion,
desire to have need of man's cooperation,
and who link him to the works of Your love,
accomplish in us what You Yourself expect of us.

❧

For a Receptive Heart
Since sanctity is a disposition of heart,
my God, make my heart an open vase.

May it be ready, waiting, abandoned
to the initiatives and to the invasion
of Your tenderness.

Thanksgiving for My Nothingness

Thank you,
Ocean of love,
for having subjected my nothingness
to Your creative fiat
and to Your actions alone.

Prayer to Prepare for Death

My God,
grant that I may say yes
to Your loving actions concerning
the circumstances of my death
so that I may have a death of love,
a death produced by Your
love acting in me.

Descending Fire

❦

A Second Prayer to Prepare for Death
Holy Trinity, I beseech you to let overflow
into my soul the streams of merciful love
that are contained in You.
May these streams consume me
without ceasing, that I may become the
victim, the martyr, and that they might
spread over me until they make me die.

❦

Prayer to the Holy Angels
Angels of God, pure lights and pure flames,
give to my wretchedness the ardor of your love,
and since you do not have the privilege of suffering,
take in exchange my trials and my death.

❦

Prayer to Obtain Love of Neighbor
Jesus, who has commanded us
to love our neighbor as You love him,

may You Yourself love this neighbor in me.
may I love him, then, with Your own love.

༄

Universal Prayer
My God,

who has permitted these times of persecution,
let the intensity of love replace its vast expanse,
the height of the flame replace the number of fires,
and make its burning heat equal to the
perilous dangers of the entire world.

༄

Prayer for the Perfection of Every Action
My God,

transform my actions into
Your scorned tenderness, in which
will be found the soul of all suffering,
the light and the flame of all death,
the perfection of every imperfect action,
the love song of every soulless creature.

Descending Fire

⚜

The Love Song of Soulless Creatures
Animals, vegetables, minerals, creatures of love
who, on the day when the Word assumed
a material body, were called to become
a hymn of pure fire, sing perfectly the
love of the Creator, by the voice and
the heart of man united to Christ.

⚜

A Prayer of the Apostle
Jesus, Mary, fill my hand with the food
that you reserve for Your sheep.
and without leaving Your arms,
without turning my head,
I will give to each one what You wish.

⚜

A Second Prayer of the Apostle
Jesus, make me delight in
preaching in the desert,

in seeing fruits fall before they are ripe,
in perceiving in them the air of death,
since they bear within themselves
the mystery of love.

※

For the Present Moment
So that I may please You always,
O my God, allow me to be completely
attentive to each present moment,
because each instant is an act of Your love
and will be, on my part, a
response to Your attentions.

※

Upon Rising
Thank You, my God, for this night.
we offer You all the actions of this day.
May they be a single act, Your unique act of love.
Take from me the liberty of displeasing You,
and compel me to please You in everything.

Descending Fire

✤

At the Time of Sleep

I sleep but my heart watches;
My heart is totally transformed in
Your misunderstood love,
universal like the Mystical Body of Christ,
perpetual like the love that
You expect from it.

✤

Only Flames

In the heart of Your child,
O Father, stir up only flames,
for the sake of the whole Mystical Body.

*St. Thérèse's Act of Oblation
to Merciful Love*

On the ninth day of June, the feast of the Most Holy Trinity, in the year of grace, 1895, St. Thérèse of Lisieux offered herself as a victim of holocaust to God's merciful love, using the following words:

> O my God! Most Blessed Trinity, I desire to love You and make You loved, to work for the glory of Holy Church by saving souls on earth and liberating those suffering in Purgatory. I desire to accomplish Your will perfectly and to reach the degree of glory You have prepared for me in Your Kingdom. I desire, in a word, to be a saint, but I feel my helplessness, and I beg You, O my God, to be Yourself my sanctity.

Descending Fire

Since You loved me so much as to give me Your only Son as my Savior and my Spouse, the infinite treasures of His merits are mine. I offer them to You with gladness, begging You to look upon me only in the Face of Jesus and in His Heart burning with love.

I offer You, too, all the merits of the saints in Heaven and on earth, their acts of love and those of the holy angels. Finally, I offer You, O Blessed Trinity, the love and merits of the Blessed Virgin, my dear Mother. It is to her that I abandon my offering, begging her to present it to You.

Her Divine Son, my beloved Spouse, told us in the days of His mortal life, "All that you ask the Father in my name He will give it to you."[72] I am certain, then, that You will grant my desires; I know, O my God, that the more You want to give, the more You make us desire.

[72] John 16:23.

I feel in my heart immense desires, and it is with confidence that I ask You to come and take possession of my soul. Ah, I cannot receive Holy Communion as often as I desire, but, Lord, are You not all-powerful? Remain in me as in a tabernacle, and never separate Yourself from Your little host.

I want to console You for the ingratitude of the wicked, and I beg of You to take away my freedom to displease You. If through weakness I sometimes fall, may Your divine glance cleanse my soul immediately, consuming all my imperfections like the fire that transforms everything into itself.

I thank You, O my God, for all the graces You have granted me, especially the grace of making me pass through the crucible of suffering. It is with joy that I shall contemplate You on the last day carrying the scepter of the Cross. Since You deigned to give me a share in this very precious Cross, I hope in Heaven to resemble You and to see shining in my glorified body the sacred stigmata of Your Passion.

Descending Fire

After earth's exile, I hope to go and enjoy You in my true home, but I do not want to lay up merits for Heaven. I want to work for Your love alone for the single purpose of pleasing You, consoling Your Sacred Heart, and saving souls who will love You eternally.

In the evening of this life, I shall appear before You with empty hands, for I do not ask You, Lord, to count my works. All our justice is stained in Your eyes. I wish, then, to be clothed in Your own justice, and to receive from Your love the eternal possession of Yourself. I want no other throne, no other crown but You, my Beloved!

Time is nothing in Your eyes; a single day is like a thousand years.[73] You can, then, in one instant prepare me to appear before You.

In order to live in a single act of perfect love, I offer myself as a victim of holocaust to Your

[73]Cf. Ps. 90:4.

merciful love, asking You to consume me incessantly, allowing the waves of infinite tenderness which are pent up within You to overflow into my soul, so that I may thus become a martyr of Your love, O my God.

May this martyrdom, after having prepared me to appear before You, finally cause me to die, and may my soul take its flight without any delay into the eternal embrace of Your merciful love.

I desire, O my Beloved, at each beat of my heart to renew this offering an infinite number of times, until, the shadows having disappeared, I may be able to tell You of my love in an eternal face-to-face.

Sophia Institute Press®

✻

Sophia Institute™ is a nonprofit institution that seeks to restore man's knowledge of eternal truth, including man's knowledge of his own nature, his relation to other persons, and his relation to God. Sophia Institute Press® serves this end in numerous ways: it publishes translations of foreign works to make them accessible for the first time to English-speaking readers; it brings out-of-print books back into print; and it publishes important new books that fulfill the ideals of Sophia Institute™. These books afford readers a rich source of the enduring wisdom of mankind.

Sophia Institute Press® makes these high-quality books available to the general public by using advanced technology and by soliciting donations to subsidize its general publishing costs. Your generosity can help Sophia Institute Press® to provide the public with editions of works containing the enduring wisdom of the ages. Please send your tax-deductible contribution to the address below. We also welcome your questions, comments, and suggestions.

For your free catalog, call:
Toll-free: 1-800-888-9344

or write:
Sophia Institute Press®
Box 5284, Manchester, NH 03108

or visit our website:
www.sophiainstitute.com

Sophia Institute™ is a tax-exempt institution
as defined by the Internal Revenue Code,
Section 501(c)(3). Tax I.D. 22-2548708.